How to Build
Strong Faith
For Your Desires

The foundation for the miraculous

Samuel O. Orefuwa

All scripture quotations are from The King James Version of the bible except stated

Direct quotations from the bible are in italics.

All rights reserved

Building Strong Faith

ISBN 978-0-6399827-0-0

Copyright 2018

Samuel O. Orefuwa

All rights reserved. No portion of this book maybe reproduced without written permission from the publisher.

For further information & permission write to
Word of Faith Media & Publications
311 Arcadia Centre
179 Steve Biko Rd
Arcadia
Pretoria
0083
Republic of South Africa

info@wof-ministries.com
www.wof-ministries.com

Index

Chapter 1 - Understanding faith

Chapter 2 - Character of strong faith

Chapter 3 - Believe the truthfulness of the Word of God

Chapter 4 - The Holy Ghost in you

Chapter 5 - Good Gifts come from Heaven

Chapter 6 - You were redeemed

Chapter 7 - Hold fast to your confession of faith

Chapter 8 - Fellowship with Christ

Chapter 9 - Faith in the name of Jesus.

Chapter 1
Understanding faith

So then faith cometh by hearing, and hearing by the word of God. **Romans 10:17**

If you have an understanding of anything, you will be able to benefit from it and put it to use skilfully. An understanding of the subject of faith will empower you to enjoy the glorious benefits that faith brings i.e. receiving your heart's desires.

God has spoken in His word that faith pleases Him and without it, you cannot please Him. But without faith it is impossible to please Him: for he that cometh to God must believe that He is, and that He is a rewarder of them that diligently seek Him (Hebrews 11:6). Christ in His early walk responded to men and women who demonstrated their faith in Him. There were instances where the power of God came out of Christ by faith, exercised by recipients of that power without Him praying for them, neither was

He aware of the conditions of the recipients of God's healing power. Whenever faith is displayed, God has put spiritual laws in motion for miracle power to flow out of the realm of the spirit. Our understanding of faith is key to seeing Christ's glorious power in manifestation on the earth; in the order of Abraham's testimony.

The encounter between Jesus and the centurion:

And when Jesus was entered into Capernaum, there came unto Him a centurion, beseeching Him,

And saying, Lord, my servant lieth at home sick of the palsy, grievously tormented.

And Jesus saith unto Him, I will come and heal him.

The centurion answered and said, Lord, I am not worthy that thou shouldest come under my roof: but speak the word only, and my servant shall be healed.

For I am a man under authority, having solders under me: and I say to this man, go, and he goeth; and to another, come, and he cometh; and to my servant, do this, and he doeth it. When Jesus heard it, He marvelled, and said to them that followed, Verily I say unto you, I have not found so great faith, no, not in Israel.

And I say unto you, that many shall come from the east and west, and shall sit down with Abraham, and Isaac, and Jacob, in the kingdom of heaven.

How to build strong Faith

But the children of the kingdom shall be cast out into outer darkness: there shall be weeping and gnashing of teeth.

And Jesus said unto the centurion Go thy way; and as though hast believed so be it done unto thee. And his servant was healed in the selfsame hour. **Matthew 8:5-13**

Jesus Christ was flabbergasted at the understanding of the Centurion concerning the authority of Christ's word when Jesus replied "*...I have not found so great faith, no, not in Israel*". What made Jesus say this was when the Centurion said "*...I am not worthy that thou shouldest come under my roof; but speak the word only and my servant shall be healed*".

The Centurion being a military man understood exercising authority through words because he himself was subject to the authority that put him in charge of soldiers and with the command of words he commanded his soldiers. In essence he understood the authority of Christ's words over sicknesses and diseases and this understanding granted him the miracle he desired. Your understanding of the subject of faith is crucial to receiving the miracle blessings you desire. God gains nothing by withholding a blessing from you. For Jesus Christ died and went through the agony of pain with shedding His blood for you that you may have access to the blessings of heaven. Satan has twisted many minds making them believe that God is against them, wants them sick, poor, unmarried, homeless and in pain.

Friends it will be done to you as you believe, *Jesus said, go thy way; and as thou hast believed, so be it done unto thee* **(Matthew 8:13)**. What you believe is key to having your heart's desires met, it happened to Abraham and it was done to him as he believed. The Bible says, *'Even so faith, if it hath not works, is dead, being alone. For as the body without the spirit is dead, so faith without works is dead also.'* **(James 2:17 & 26)**

Many in the body of Christ boast of having faith but we don't see the results of their faith, because they do not understand the subject of faith. Apostle James says, having faith is not enough, your faith must have proofs, works and actions corresponding to your faith, if not then your faith is dead, will be unfruitful, unproductive and it will not draw God's attention at all. Just as the body without the spirit has no life, but dead, so also is faith without actions or corresponding behaviour that proves your faith. This can be further stressed by saying if you believe you are healed then behave healed and if you believe you are rich then behave rich. Until you behave what you believe, what you believe will not generate the results your desire.

And as He entered into a certain village, there met

him ten men that were lepers, which stood afar off: And they lifted up their voices, and said, Jesus, Master, have mercy on us. And when he saw them, He said unto them, Go shew yourselves unto the priests. And it came to pass, that, as they went, they were cleansed. **Luke 17: 12-14**

These lepers must have heard of Jesus healing other lepers because as soon as they saw Jesus they cried unto Him out of their colony, as lepers were kept outside the village away from the community according to the law concerning leprosy in Leviticus 13:13-14. When Jesus saw them He didn't pray for them but told them to go show themselves unto the priests. Why didn't He pray for them or touch them but just gave them an instruction to obey? According to the law in Leviticus 13:13 -14, no leper should enter the village to see the priest except you have been confirmed cleansed. When Jesus told them to go and show themselves to the priest, He wanted to teach them something about faith and what faith in His words can do. He was demanding the behaviour that demonstrates faith from them.

Jesus knew the law that only those who are healed can enter the village to show up before the priest. When He instructed them to go show themselves to the priest it was to give them the opportunity to demonstrate their faith in Him. As far as Christ was concerned they were healed and He gave that instruction to them to act upon consequent to their believing that they were healed and if they believe they must appear before the priest.

The lepers obeyed Christ's instruction without arguing about what the law concerning leprosy says. Though the instruction looked stupid and foolish because they were not healed before the instruction was given, they acted on that instruction because of their faith. They behaved as though they were healed and embarked upon the journey to see the priest. The bible says "...as they went, they were cleansed." Their faith behaviour triggered the healing power of God to cleanse them of leprosy, Glory to God!

Your faith is behaving the word of God, the instructions of God or the settled facts of God. God responds to faith and if He can respond to the faith of these ten lepers then He will respond to your faith. Seek Him for His word to act on or behave and enjoy the great and marvellous miracle power of God. With this understanding of faith let us look at the character of strong faith so that you will know what it looks like. If you don't have it then you can begin to build into your spirit the qualities of strong faith that cause God to do marvellous things on the earth. God wants to reverse the irreversible, do the incredible, pour out His blessings and bring great changes in people's lives but strong faith is required.

Chapter 2
Character of strong faith

(As it is written, I have made thee a father of many nations,) before him whom he believed, even God, who quickeneth the dead, and calleth those things which be not as though they were.

Who against hope believed in hope, that he might become the father of many nations, according to that which was spoken, So shall they seed be.

And being not weak in faith, he considered not his own body now dead, when he was about an hundred years old, neither yet the deadness of Sara's womb:

He staggered not at the promise of God through unbelief but was STRONG IN FAITH, giving glory to God. **Romans 4:17-20**

Building strong faith is a necessity if you are going to see God move in your life, meeting your needs with His power. We live in a time whereby we all want to see God at work on the earth but this will require us to show Him our strong faith. You will need to build the qualities of strong faith into your spirit, so that Christ's power may be in manifestation in your life to have bodies healed, financial needs met, marital needs met, souls poured into the kingdom, large churches built and to see God's glory on the earth like never before.

The scripture above referred to Abraham's faith, a description of his faith after God told him he would yet still have a son even after his wife Sarah had reached menopause and was old, making it naturally impossible for her to conceive, but it was the strength of Abraham's faith that caused God to do as He had told him. Abraham 'being not weak in faith, he considered not his own body now dead, when he was about an hundred years old, neither yet the deadness of Sara's womb. What are the qualities of strong faith as described by the word of God in Abraham? We see that Abraham's strong faith caused him to be hopeful when there was no hope. The hope of having a child was bleak and dark because there was no chance for him in the natural but yet Abraham believed in Hope, he had an expectation that he would have a child according to what God had told him. In the midst of the darkness of barrenness, his expectation was based on the light provided by God's word to him hence he agreed to change his name to father of all nations, ABRAHAM, and had people call him by that name every day.

1. Strong faith is hopeful

Strong faith is that faith that is full of hope against all hope when there is no reason in the natural for you to be hopeful, but you are expectant and you go further to show that you believe in hope by preparing for your expectations. When a barren woman is buying clothes for her expectant babies, that is hope against all hope, and it pleases the Lord to see you exercise your strong faith in this manner.

Years ago, I told a lady who was believing God to be married to buy a shirt for her husband to be. I asked her 'do you have a picture of how your husband will be?' She replied 'yes'. I then told her to go and buy him a shirt and talk to that shirt everyday and thank God for causing her husband to come and put on his shirt. She did and after 8 months a young man showed up and they got married in our church in Johannesburg. Strong faith is being full of expectation without any reason for expectation but God.

2. Strong faith gives no attention to contrary circumstances

From Abraham's character strong faith is that faith that does not consider the circumstances that are contrary to what you believe, Abraham considered not his own body now dead neither yet the deadness of Sarah's womb. He never looked at the condition of his body neither that of his wife's, that is the character of strong faith it does not give attention to contrary circumstances. Strong faith is that which does not consider contrary circumstances but is one that fixes his gaze and mind on the word of God. The strength of strong faith is in the word from God that you fix your eyes on, that you meditated upon, and give daily attention to. Abraham spoke the word of God daily, moment by moment and spoke it to himself also so that his mind may not interfere with his heart's believe.

3. Strong faith is based on God's integrity

He staggered not at the promise of God thorough unbelief; but was strong in faith, giving glory to God. **(Roman 4:20)**. Abraham did not stagger i.e. he did not wonder nor let his mind wonder about what God had told him, he fixed his gaze on the word from God. Strong faith also believes in the integrity and power of God and counts it done once God has spoken. And being fully persuaded that, what he had promised, he was able also to perform **(Romans 4:21)**. Abraham believed God because he knew the integrity of God that once He says it, He will do it and that He is also capable of doing whatever He promised by His power. Having walked with God in close relationship he had developed trust in God, that He is faithful, He has integrity and by His power, His word will come to pass no matter the contrary circumstances.

4. Strong faith gives glory to God

Having now counted it done based on the word from God, strong faith exhibits its greatest quality by giving glory, thanks and worship to God for what He has said and done in His word. Strong faith must exhibit this character if it is to be called strong faith, it must worship God a lot, thanking Him for what He has done that has not yet been seen as done. This is where we distinguish weak faith from strong faith, especially when the manifestation of that which is promised is delayed. Most people give up when that which is promised seems late to manifest because the strength of their faith is weak. Strong faith does not cower but rather it weathers down every storm of unbelief and doubt by standing strong on the word from God irrespective of the hopelessness of the situation.

Strong faith is a stubborn faith that does not yield nor give up easily; it maintains the confessions of the word received from God, gives thanks for it and is full of expectations in the midst of darkness and hopelessness.

5. Strong faith is a product of relationship with God

You cannot believe with people that have weak faith,

if you do, most people will drop you on your journey of faith when what is promised is delayed. You have to believe yourself; this is why strong faith is a product of your personal walk with God; your fellowship, your study of the word, your prayer life, your service to Him, your journey of faith, your experiences with Him, your encounters and visitations of God. What do you desire? What are you believing God for? What is it that men say is impossible? Friend, you only need the word of God, which is the Rhema word that you receive from an encounter with Him, which you can use to produce strong faith. With strong faith, you will watch as God manifests in your life to reverse the irreversible, do the impossible and meet your heart's desires.

Years ago fertility doctors in London and South Africa told my wife that they cannot help her, that her womb was messed up in a previous fibroid operation she had and declared NO HOPE. They suggested we go for surrogacy, but I have a covenant with God and His word is my covenant therefore I sought God for several years on this matter. Then one day I decided I need to settle this matter with God therefore I gathered scriptures on fruitfulness and began to pray for several days until suddenly after about 7 days, I fell into a trance and an angel appeared to me and brought my wife before me and told me, 'we have put a seed in her womb, this is how to pray for her'.

After that encounter I called my wife, anointed her womb as I was told and kept declaring the seed is in her. After a week or so my wife called me to confirm that she thinks she's pregnant, then another journey of faith started because throughout her pregnancy she was still seeing her period. Two doctors did not see any baby in her womb but a fibroid until my son was born. It was my wife's strong faith to believe she was pregnant for nine months; she kept on believing she was pregnant until the six month when her stomach began to protrude. We stood on what the angel said irrespective of doctors or men's report until my son was born. Glory to God!

Chapter 3
Believe the truthfulness of the Word of God

The Word is the truth

The word of God is the revelation from God to us of Himself, what He has done, who we are, what we have, His plan and purpose in Christ. The word of God is the TRUTH i.e. the reality which is the absolute TRUTH. When you believe the truthfulness of God's word any situation that is contrary to His word you can declare as false. *Sanctify them through thy truth: thy word is truth.* **(John 17:17)**

The Greek word for truth is 'aletheia', which means 'reality, the manifested, unconcealed essence of a matter'. To sanctify means set apart, Jesus prayed to the Father to set us apart from the evil of the world by His TRUTH and the word of God is that TRUTH. Building strong faith requires you to believe in the absolute truthfulness of God's word. Whatever is written in the bible or He says to you about anything in your life is the truth, the reality and any other thing contrary to what He says to you is false and cannot stand. *Heaven and earth shall pass away, but my words shall not pass away. (John 8:32 KJV). And ye shall know the TRUTH, and the truth shall make you free.* **(Matthew 24:35 KJV)**

The Word is the reality

God's word which is the truth, the reality, the indisputable fact, has been given to free you from the bondages and the oppressive forces of this world. God's word is what causes Him to show up on the earth, His word is the covenant He has made with His people. The word of God will stand the test of time; circumstances and situations will pass away but God's word will stand forever, for it is infallible, dependable and reliable in any situation. *Thy word is true from the beginning* **(Psalm 119:16).** *Forever, O Lord, thy word is settled in heaven.* **(Psalm 119:89).** God's word is genuine and pure unlike man's word that can be flawed, corrupted and contaminated. *Thy word is very pure: therefore thy servant loveth it* **(Psalm 119:140).** Due to the reliability, infallibility and genuineness of the word of God, you should feed on it, think of it daily until it gets into your spirit and helps you become strong in the Lord, thereby building very strong faith against oppositions or whatever situation you are faced with.

Just feed on the word of God until it becomes a part of your being that controls and rules you. Except you are established in the reality of God's word, you can be overtaken by lies and the falsehood in the environment where you are. The word of God is neither subject to scientific reviews nor philosophical research, *Beware lest any man spoil you through philosophy and vain deceit, after the tradition of men, after the rudiments of the world, and not after Christ.* **(Colossians 2:8)**.

To be ignorant is to be robbed, and man's word and philosophical opinion will rob you of the reality of the word of God that frees men from the oppression of the devil. Building strong faith in God requires knowing the reality and infallibility of His word. You can only depend on His word because it is the TRUTH, no one seeks to depend on falsehood. Strengthen your faith with God's word. Reading, studying, sharing, proclaiming Gods words unleashes power that can demolish the lying opposition.

Poverty, lack and insufficiency are not our reality as believers. Plenty and abundance is our reality, God is our source. He is the God of plenty and abundance and we that are in HIM were born into abundance and plenty. *Therefore is any man be in Christ, he is a new creature:*

old things are passed away; behold, all things are become new **(2 Corinthians 5:17)**. Believers were born into a family of wealth, the family of Abraham. We that are in Christ are in the blessing of Abraham; the blessing of Abraham is our reality and the blessing is working in us to make us rich. That's the truth, for the word of God is the reality of a believer. So with this truth you can stand against the lies of poverty, lack and insufficiency

The Word is the blessing

The blessings of the Lord, it maketh rich, and He added no sorrow to it **(Proverbs 10:22 KJV)**, the blessing of the Lord on Abraham made him rich and the same anointing has been made available to us by Christ's sacrifice of himself. *Christ had redeemed us from the curse of the law, being made a curse for us: for it is written, Cursed is every one that hangeth on a tree.* **(Galatians 3:13 KJV)**. You have been redeemed from the curse of poverty, lack and insufficiency, that's the truth that you need to make part of you until you have no sense of lack. We are not needy people but blessed people of God. *Thou shall be blessed above all people: there shall not be male or female barren among you or among your cattle* **(Deuteronomy 7:14)**.

Make the blessing your reality and not the curse, be blessing conscious, it is your inheritance. *And if ye be in Christ, then are ye Abraham's seed, and HEIRS according to the promise.* **(Galatians 3:29).** *Know ye therefore that truly which one of FAITH, the same are the children of ABRAHAM.* **(Galatians 3:7 KJV),** thank God, Abraham's blessing is ours! There is an abundant provision for us in Christ we are blessed with plenty of everything. *And the Lord shall make thee plenteous in goods, in the fruit of the body, and in the fruit of thy cattle, and in the fruit of thy ground, in the land which the LORD sware unto thy fathers to give thee.* **(Deuteronomy 28:11 KJV)**

The Word is the healer

Sicknesses and diseases are not to rule and reign over you. You are to reign over sicknesses and diseases and destroy their presence in your body with the truth of God's word. *That it might be fulfilled which was spoken by Esaias the prophet, saying, Himself took our infirmities, and bare our sicknesses.* **(Matthew 8:17 KJV).** The reality is that He took your sicknesses and diseases therefore whatever is causing pain in your body is a lie. That diabetes, HIV and cancer in your body is a lie! The truth is that Christ took them away and all you have to do is to command Satan to take his hands off your body, resist him by the blood of Jesus. As you confess the truth of God's word and resist the lies of the devil you will cause the word to be the reality of your life. Believing with your heart the truth and confessing it with your

How to build strong Faith

mouth will cause your faith muscles to be strong because only strong faith will provoke the miraculous in your life especially with impossible situations.

Chapter 4
The Holy Ghost in you

When you know that the Holy Ghost dwells in you, it makes a great difference in your walk of faith. It strengthens your faith because He is the power source of that miracle or change you desire. *Know ye not that your body is the temple of the Holy Ghost which is in you, which ye have of God, and ye are not your own? For ye are bought with a price, therefore glorify God in your body and in your spirit which are God's.* **1 Corinthians 6:19.**

Ye are of God, little children, and have overcome them: because greater is He that is in you, than he that is in the world. **1 John 4.4**

The Holy Ghost, the third person of the Godhead lives in you and He is greater than anything or any circumstance in this world. Knowing this truth will strengthen your faith and confession. When you challenged with impossibility, you must say 'the greater one is in me; He makes me greater than this impossible situation; He makes me the head over this matter; He causes me to overcome the opposition; He reverses the irreversible for me; He is removing every opposition out of my way; He is greater than every opposition in the world!'

THE PURPOSE OF THE HOLY GHOST

It takes revelation of the purpose of the Holy Ghost in you to be able to make these kinds of confessions. The Holy Ghost is your helper, thank God for the Holy Ghost. I have received the help of the Holy Ghost in many helpless situations I found myself in. I turned to Him and talked to Him saying: 'please Holy Spirit help me, I don't know what to do here, I'm weak I can't even preach'. Whenever I talked to God on the inside of me this way He comes out with solutions all the time, He helped me every time I asked Him. I'm telling you He is your helper!

THE HOLY GHOST IS THE HELPER

I was in Canada to preach and before my meeting I felt sick and tired, I tried to pray but my body felt sick, I turned to Him to heal my body and to help me that night to be able to stand all night and preach. As soon as the microphone was given to me the Holy Spirit took over, strength came to me and I ministered in the power of the

Holy Ghost. I was healed and so many people were also healed. *Let your conversation be without covetousness, and be content with such things as ye have: for He hath said, I will never leave thee, nor forsake thee. So that we may boldly say, The Lord is my helper, and I will not fear what man shall do unto me.* **Hebrews 13:5-6 KJV.**

Submit to The Holy Ghost, s*ubmit yourselves therefor to God. Resist the devil, and he will flee from you.* **(James 4:7).** We are instructed in the word of God to submit to God, the God inside our spirit, He who is in your spirit to lead and guide you in this life. He knows about the situation more than you can ever fathom. *For as many as are led by the Spirit of God, they are the sons of God.* **(Romans 8:14).** When you allow Him that is on the inside of you to lead you, you will enjoy His help, miracles, favour and blessings and even if He leads you into difficult situations, He will still give you grace to pull through. When you are faced with opposition, don't cry, don't panic, He that is on the inside of you will put you over every opposition and obstacle.

His leading, His directions and instructions should be the foundation for your faith whereby you believe that it shall be even as He has told you.

THE HOLY GHOST IS THE POWER SOURCE

The Holy Spirit is the power source; all of the power needed to succeed and be victorious in this life is already in you by virtue of the Holy Spirit being in you. *But ye shall receive power, after that the Holy Ghost is come upon you: and ye shall be witnesses unto me both in Jerusalem, and in all Judaea, and in Samaria, and unto the uttermost part of the earth.* **Acts 1:8**

Know that inside of you is all the power you need to heal you, prosper you and put you over that impossible situation. The Holy Ghost is in you in all His fullness, believe it, know it and act as though that power is working in you. Confess that the power of God is working in you to heal you, bless you and destroy the power of the enemy against you. *But if the Spirit of Him that raised up Jesus from the dead dwell in you, He that raised up Christ from the dead shall also quicken your mortal bodies by His Spirit that dwelleth in you.* **Romans 8:11.**

Knowing the truth of the scripture will cause your body to be filled with God's healing power and the life of Jesus that makes your body strong and healthy. The spirit of God in you shall pour life into your body if you will ask Him by faith and command your body to be made strong by the power of the Spirit resident in your spirit, He will be poured out from your spirit into your body.

Anytime I feel tired, I ask the Spirit to fill my body with the life and power of God. I command every cell in my body to be filled with the life of God and be healthy in Jesus name. Anytime I do this I wake up strong and healthy no matter how tired I was the previous night. Know that the Spirit of God is in the inside of you, be conscious of His presence and take advantage of His power resident in your spirit.

Chapter 5
Good Gifts come from Heaven

There is no evil in Heaven. Heaven is a place of peace, joy, life, blessings, light and love that God has prepared for His children. God has prepared good and perfect gifts to bless you beyond your wildest dreams. God's blessings are here, prepared for them that believe. *"Every good gift and every perfect gift is from above, and cometh down from the Father of lights, with whom is no variableness, neither shadow of turning"* **James 1:17 KJV.**

God has no evil to give His own but blessings for He is a God of love, joy, peace and blessings. His love drove Christ to the cross to make all that is of God available to you. *'He that spared not His own Son, but delivered Him up for us all, how shall He not with Him also freely give us all things?'* **(Romans 8:32).** God has neither sickness nor disease to give you, He doesn't give poverty,

He is not responsible for lack and your knowledge of this will help you stand strong against the enemy, Satan, who is the source of evil in this world.

Jesus said Satan was the one who bound the woman with a spinal condition for Eighteen years,

And aught not this woman, being a daughter of Abraham, whom satan hath bound, lo, these eighteen years, be loosed from this bond on the Sabbath day? **(Luke 13:16 KJV)**

Satan was the one that stole from Job all that God had blessed him with but Job didn't know this and so he thought it was God who was responsible for his calamity. *"So went Satan forth from the presence of the LORD, and smote Job with sore boils from the sole of his foot unto his crown".* **(Job 2:7)**. *Though He slay me, yet will I trust in Him: but I will maintain mine own ways before Him.* **(Job 13:15)**. God was not responsible for his calamities, it was Satan who attacked his family, business and health but God who is the restorer was the one who restored back all that the enemy stole from Job. *"So the LORD blessed the latter end of Job more than his beginning: for he had fourteen thousand sheep, and six thousand camels, and a thousand yoke of oxen, and a thousand she asses"..***(Job 42:10)**. God is a restorer and the blesser and not the destroyer. Every destruction you see in this world is caused by Satan, he is the thief, killer and destroyer. *The thief cometh not, but for to steal, and to kill, and to destroy: I am come that they might have life, and that they might have it more abundantly.* **(John 10:10).**

When Satan enters people's lives he ruins their lives and causes them to commit suicide, be poor, sick and diseased. He enters families and tears them apart resulting in divorce and emotional pain, makes countries desolate. *"That made the world as a wilderness, and destroyed the cities thereof, that opened not the house of his prisoners?"* **(Isaiah 14:17).** The knowledge of the source of evil causes you to stand strong against the enemy with your faith. If God was responsible for your problems, how then will you be able to stand against God? Your faith will be so weak you will just accept the situation as it is.

CHAPTER 6
YOU WERE REDEEMED

"Christ hath redeemed us from the curse of the law, being made a curse for us: for it is written, Cursed is every one that hangeth on a tree: **Ephesians 1:7 KJV** *In whom we have redemption through His blood, the forgiveness of sins, according to the riches of His grace".* **Galatians 3:13**

The word 'redeem' means 'to buy out'. The term was used in reference to the purchase of slaves' freedom in ancient times. The application of this term to Christ's sacrifice implies we were once under a slave master, the devil, who kept us under captivity from the time of Adam when he sinned against God thereby handing over rulership of this world to Satan. In redemption a price or a ransom must be paid to obtain release of the slave and in our redemption Christ was the ransom (price) for our release, **Galatians 3:13** says *'Christ has redeemed us,*

. chased us from the hold of the slave master, the devil, by making Himself a curse'. We are no longer slaves to Satan who is the source of sin, pain, agony, poverty, sicknesses and diseases. Christ Jesus offered Himself as the sacrifice, died and poured out his blood under pain and agony to break Satan's hold over us. Glory to GOD!

We are free! The ransom has been paid! He is the Christ, the RANSOM, the Gift to the World, the chosen Redeemer; He is the gift to the sinners, great gift to the sick, the blind, the poor, and the broken-hearted. *'In whom we have redemption through His blood...' therefore His blood was the price paid for the redemption from the hold of the devil, as a result we are free from sin, sickness, disease, poverty, evil, sorrow and rejection.* "*Giving thanks unto the Father, which hath made us meet to be partakers of the inheritance of the saints in light: Who hath delivered us form the power of darkness, and hath translated us into the kingdom of His dear Son: In whom we have redemption through His blood, even the forgiveness of sins*". **Colossians 1:12-14 KJV.**

Apostle Paul was writing to the Church at Colossae and brought forth a revelation of what the Father had done in Christ by saying 'we give thanks to the Father of our Lord Jesus Christ who hath(has) made us meet(qualified) to partake (share, participate) in the inheritance of Saints in light'.

These inheritances are as follows:

Who hath delivered us from the power of darkness.

We are saints in light, free from the hold of the power of darkness and this was made possible when Christ paid with His blood, the ransom price for our freedom. We have been delivered from Satan's hold of evil, sickness, disease, poverty, demons, evil spirits and their host. *"Let the redeemed of the LORD say so, whom He hath redeemed from the hand of the enemy"*. **(Psalm 107:2).** You have to maintain a daily confession of what happened to you in Christ. You have been delivered from the authority of darkness, they have no authority over you and you have left their camp when the price of redemption was paid. Maintain a strong confession of this for the knowledge of this truth is your foundation for strong faith against the enemy of poverty, sickness and disease.

Build on the truth and it will produce strong faith in you which will produce the results you desire thereby meeting your needs, bringing God's power into manifestation to heal your body and destroy the oppression of the devil.

We have been redeemed from poverty, sickness, and diseases.

You don't have to be poor or sick again! God's riches are on the earth, and they are for you so claim them as yours and command Satan to take his hands off your finances in Jesus name because the price for your financial freedom has been paid.

Daily confess Christ has redeemed me from poverty by His blood. I am free from poverty therefore I claim financial abundance in Jesus name. You are the custodian of your body and Satan has lost his hold over the human body because the Blood of Christ has bought you from the hold of Satan. The human body has been freed and you don't have to be oppressed in your body anymore, your body belongs to God.

What? Know ye not that your body is the temple of the Holy Ghost which is in you, which ye have of God, and ye are not your own? For ye are bought with a price: therefore glorify God in your body, and in your spirit, which are God's. **(1 Corinthians 6:19-20)**. Your body has become home to the Holy Spirit, making it His temple, a place to dwell in. Christ paid the price for the redemption of your body, so that the Holy Spirit may come in with God's healing power to make your body strong and healthy. Know this truth, be conscious of it and ask Him to fill you with God's power. Satan's power to hold your body in sickness has been destroyed, therefore if you are told you have HIV or cancer don't panic but rather tell the Holy Ghost: this is Your body and I refuse that it be filled with Satan's diseases, fill me with Your healing power. I claim Your power in me, in Jesus name! Cancer or HIV I command you to die in my body. DIE! And wither away in Jesus name!

For verily I say unto you, That whosoever shall say unto this mountain, Be thou removed, and be thou cast into the sea; and shall not doubt in his heart, but shall believe that those things which he saith shall come to pass; he shall have whatsoever he saith. **(Mark 11:23)**. What are those mountains you are faced with? You have been redeemed from them, confront them with scriptures and speak to them to disappear, to be cut off and wither away. Jesus said, 'speak to the mountain', therefore do not speak to God about the mountain but confront the mountain in Jesus name! God has given you authority to take care of your body, you are the custodian of your body therefore make it glorify God. Sickness does not glorify God but being healthy and strong does glorify God.

CHAPTER 7
HOLD FAST TO YOUR CONFESSION OF FAITH

Let us hold fast the profession of our faith without wavering; (for He is faithful that promised) **Hebrews 10:23**. Your faith muscles when exercised strengthen just as your flesh muscles strengthen when you exercise them. Faith muscles are made strong when exercised regularly and consistently. Many people's faith muscles are weak because they are not exercised regularly, when faced with an emergency they want to speak faith a little and get results and it doesn't work that way. You must practice and exercise your faith daily. When things are well and when you don't need a miracle. To hold fast to your profession of faith is to keep confessing what you believe consistently without giving up in the face of any opposition. Keeping your confession of faith strong means to consistently say what you believe and to believe what you say until the opposing forces are blasted out of the way.

Get a scripture for what you are believing God for then apply it to your life, the scriptures that promise you your heart's desires. Keep confessing that scripture, personalize the scripture, put yourself in the scripture, see yourself with solutions in the scripture and confess it day and night, if possible, thousands of times a day. When you need a miracle or are faced with an emergency you need to take time out to confess what you believe, hold on to your confession until God stamps your confession approved in Heaven and once God approves your confession you will see His miracle power at work. The power of God will manifest to give you what you've been confessing.

I stood on **Mark 11:24**, *"therefore I say unto you, What things soever ye desire, whey ye pray, believe that ye receive them, and ye shall have them"*. Confessing I believe, I receive one hundred thousand rands, I stood on my confession thousands of times for years until God's power manifested and a lady gave me one hundred thousand rands. I also confessed consistently that I believe, I receive a prudent wife from God, night and day believing He will show me the prudent wife, He surely did. I saw my wife and the Holy Ghost spoke from my spirit to me 'that is your wife'. I came to South Africa as a Missionary, and got hold of **Mark 10:29-30**, *'And Jesus answered and said, Verily I say unto you, There is no man that hath left house, or brethren, or sisters, or father, or mother, or wife, or children, or lands, for my sake, and the gospel's.*

But he shall receive and hundredfold now in this time, houses, and brethren, and sisters, and mothers, and children, and lands, with persecutions; and in the world to come eternal life'.

I believed God for children, land, brothers, sisters, mothers, and fathers. I confessed the scripture regularly and I have held onto it now for years till today and I have been reaping the results as God gives me all the contents of **Mark KJV 10:30**, *"But he shall receive and hundredfold now in this time, houses, and brethren, and sisters, and mothers, and children, and lands, with persecutions; and in the world to come eternal life".* I did not give up, for He sent me and I continue to reap the harvest of souls in the land, they are mine according to Mark 10:30. I decided to claim it, and confess that the contents of Mark 10:30 are mine, I claim the land, houses, brothers, sisters, children etc, and I have seen them come to me and into our ministry.

Hold fast to your profession, your profession is to confess your faith and keep at it, exercise that faith until God stamps it approved, in Jesus name. *Death and life are in the power of the tongue: and they that love it shall eat the fruit thereof.* **(Proverbs 18:21)**. *A man's belly shall be satisfied with the fruit of his mouth; and with the increase of his lips shall he be filled.* **(Proverbs 18:20)**.

Increase of words from your lips can fill your life, your accounts, your business and anything that is empty in your life. Get a scripture that concerns your case, which provides solutions to what you need and put them on your lips repeatedly until you are filled. When the Bible says Abraham was strong in faith giving glory to God, it is saying, Abraham kept calling himself father and others also kept calling him father until he eventually became the father of Isaac. He kept his confession strong, thanking God for His word and that He was faithful who promised him a child. Judge God faithful, 'He is faithful that promised', God who gave His word to you cannot lie. He is bound by His word, He keeps His word and He never renegades on His promise; He is faithful, believe it! He will keep His promise to you as you keep His word in your mouth and keep saying it until you see the results you desire. God is faithful; He will never fail you, thank Him and give Him glory for His word to you.

Chapter 8
Fellowship with Christ

God is faithful, by whom ye were called unto the fellowship of his Son Jesus Christ our Lord. Now I beseech you, brethren, by the name of our Lord Jesus Christ, that ye all speak the same thing, and that there be no divisions among you; but that ye be perfectly joined together in the same mind and in the same judgment. **1 Corinthians 1:9-10**

Hear what the Holy Spirit is speaking through Apostle Paul saying 'believers have been called into the fellowship of Christ'. The English word for fellowship is translated from the Greek word 'koinonia', which means unity, share, participate and communicate. Believers have been called to the unity of Christ, sharing, participating and communicating with Christ and this is only possible through prayer.

Prayer is fellowshipping with God, communicating with God. In prayer, your spirit unites with that of Christ deeply, *'for he that speaketh in an unkown tongue speaketh not unto men, but unto God'* **(1 Corinthians 14:2).** Speaking in tongues is one of the signifying signs of a New Creation Believer and he who speaks in tongues speaks unto God. When praying to God the believer's spirit intermingles with God's Spirit. In prayer there is union, participation and communication, and that is the foundation for strong faith. For in prayer Christ's faith is deposited into the believer's spirit that produces the God kind of Faith that can move mountains.

Praying in tongues for long hours is recommended for those who want to build strong faith. In prayer you hear God, He gives you His word, makes known His plans to you, causes you to see the invisible which helps you to build a very strong faith. From my own experience in prayer, praying in tongues for 8 – 10 hours sometimes 18hours a day helped me to hear God, see the invisible, receive angelic visitations with a word from the LORD that helped me build strong faith for my ministry and to receive all that my ministry needs from the LORD. In 2006, while praying, having prayed in tongues for 6hours I fell into a trance and saw an angel who came to me and said 'I am from the Lord God Almighty, if you keep digging, you will find gold'. I received this message with great attention, started praying in tongues for hours daily as I was told. This act of praying became the secret of the anointing on my life and the manifestation of the Gift of Special Faith in my ministry which is the supernatural manifestation of God's faith in my life and ministry.

When at a miracle services or crusades, I always know when that Gift of Special Faith comes on me and when I yield to it we always have great miracles in the services or in our crusades.

CHAPTER 9
FAITH IN THE NAME OF JESUS

And these signs shall follow them that believe; In my name shall they cast out devils; they shall speak with new tongues; They shall take up serpents; and if they drink any deadly thing, it shall not hurt them; they shall lay hands on the sick, and they shall recover. **Mark 16:17-18**

The Lord Jesus said to His disciples to use His name to cast out devils, deal with demons and evil spirits, heal the sick by laying hands on them and no deadly drink shall hurt them because of His name. He left them this instruction just before He was received up into heaven to sit at the right hand of God. He knew what the sacrifice and price He paid had done to His name; His name has been exalted above all other names. The revelation of what has happened to His name by His death, burial, seventy-two hours in hell and resurrection had not dawned on the disciples. All the resources of heaven are now available on the earth and ready for usage through the name of Jesus. Also, Jesus Christ was ascending to heaven to take His position at the right hand of the Father, to back up anyone with the revelation of His name and make it real on the earth, as He has said to them, 'In my name they shall cast out devils; speak in new tongues...'. He was not telling them to pray now, He was giving them instructions on what His name will do henceforth, and they should just go, act on it and use it. The name has become the believer's inheritance.

And being found in fashion as a man, he humbled himself, and became obedient unto death, even the death of the cross. Wherefore God also hath highly exalted him, and given him a name which is above every name: That at the name of Jesus every knee should bow, of things in heaven, and things in earth, and things under the earth; And that every tongue should confess that Jesus Christ is Lord, to the glory of God the Father. **Philippians 2:8-11**

According to the above scriptures, God has exalted the name of Jesus above every other name, of things in heaven, and things in earth, and things under the earth. These things have been made to obey or to be subject to the name of Jesus. Jesus Christ has paid the price on the cross, and the Father has accepted His sacrifice of obedience by being slaughtered on the cross. Now the reward of His sufferings is the exaltation of His name, the name of Jesus is above every other name. It's a fact, the truth, THE REALITY! His name is above poverty, sickness, diseases, sin, cancer, failure, dollars, pounds, rands and nairas. It is above any name! Study this and you will see every name bow down before you in the name of Jesus.

The name of Jesus in Prayer

And in that day ye shall ask me nothing. Verily, verily, I say unto you, Whatsoever ye shall ask the Father in my name, he will give it you. Hitherto have ye asked nothing in my name: ask, and ye shall receive, that your joy may be full. **John 16:23-24**

Another instruction of Jesus to the disciples about using His name in prayer is that 'in that day' they will not pray to Jesus but to God the Father in the name of Jesus. Jesus Christ was telling them that a day was coming, the day of redemption, when their prayers will have to be offered to God the father and not to Jesus because at that time He would have paid the price, offered Himself for our redemption and the Father would have put all resources of heaven and earth in the hands of Jesus. 'The earth is the Lord's all the fullness thereof', 'whatsoever you ask' in the name of Jesus will be granted to you. The name of Jesus is our access to the resources of the Father and all that He has made available in Jesus Christ. Whatsoever you desire that is available in Christ is accessible through the name of Jesus. Be bold to ask the Father your heart's desires in Jesus' name. Jesus said in John 16:23-24, the Father will give you whatsoever you ask of Him and your joy will be full. It is the Father's good pleasure to answer prayers offered in the name of Jesus. You are God's child, you have the right to use the family name when making a request, in the Kingdom and our family is Jesus Christ. Ask the Father in the name of Jesus that which you desire and watch Him back you up tremendously.

Placing a demand in the name of Jesus

"And whatsoever ye shall ask in my name, that will I do, that the Father may be glorified in the Son. If ye shall ask any thing in my name, I will do it". **John 14:13-14**

All power and authority has been given to Jesus and now that same power and authority has been given to you to live and function by in His name, the name of Jesus. Everything in this world is subject to the name of Jesus, they bow to His name. In the above scripture, the word 'ask' in Greek is 'aitew' which means to demand, request or call for. Jesus was telling the disciples just before His crucifixion that whatsoever they demand, call for or request to be done in the name of Jesus, it will be done. This scripture is talking about using the power and authority of the name of Jesus in demanding or calling for things to be done, it's about using it in prayer and using it in faith in the name of Jesus; the acting force that gets Jesus to get His will done on the earth. Whatsoever He paid for through His crucifixion, death, burial and resurrection can be demanded to be done in Jesus name. Develop your faith in His name and learn to use it against the forces of darkness arranged against you in this world. Use it against poverty, sicknesses and diseases. Break the power of Satan over your life and over your loved ones.

Peter said to the lame man: *In the name of Jesus of Nazareth rise up and walk, and the man got up leaping and praising God* **Acts 3:6.**

Paul said to the spirit of divination in **Acts 16:18**, *I command you in the name of Jesus Christ to come out of her*, and the insane woman was perfectly restored. Christ has bestowed us His name, it is our inheritance. We have the right to use it. Forces of darkness in this world are subject to that name, Luke 10:17. Our faith is built on this truth.

And whatsoever ye do in word or deed, do all in the name of the Lord Jesus, giving thanks to God and the Father by him. **Colossians 3:17**

Giving thanks always for all things unto God and the

Father in the name of our Lord Jesus Christ. **Ephesians 5:20**

"... anointing him with oil <u>in the name of the Lord:</u>" **James 5:14**

And this is his commandment, that we should believe on the name of his Son Jesus Christ, and love one another, as he gave us commandment. **1 John 3:23**

In the name of Jesus demand that the mountains of finances and sicknesses to disappear and they will. How I have used this name in many of our healing crusades and conferences and seen many miracles happen as a result. I have prayed for many things asking God for supply in the name of Jesus and He has been faithful to supply them because of the name of Jesus.

OTHER BOOKS BY SAME AUTHOR

- Christ the Financier
- Gifts of Healing
- Prayer of Faith

CONTACT INFORMATION

Word of Faith Bookshop
311 Arcadia Centre
379 Steve Biko Rd
Arcadia Pretoria
0083
South Africa
Tel: 012 326 87830
info@wof-ministries.com
www.wof-ministries.com